A Willowisp
Christmas Songbook

Compiled by Margaret Holland

Illustrated by Lynn Knoll

Music arranged by John D. Mitchell

Published by Willowisp Press, Inc.
10100 SBF Drive, Pinellas Park, Florida 34666

Copyright © 1987 by Willowisp Press, Inc.   Printed in the United States of America

All rights reserved. No portion of this book may be reproduced, stored in a retrieval system, or transmitted, in any form or by any means, electronic, mechanical, photocopying, recording, or otherwise without prior written permission from the publisher.

ISBN 0-87406-253-5   10 9 8 7 6 5 4

Deck the Halls

Traditional   *Welsh*

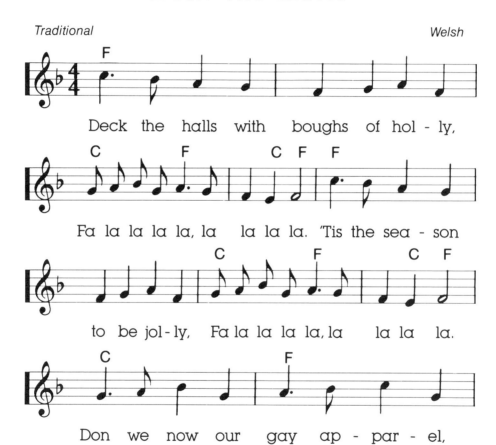

Deck the halls with boughs of hol - ly,

Fa la la la la, la   la la la. 'Tis the sea - son

to be jol - ly,   Fa la la la la, la   la la   la.

Don we now our   gay ap - par - el,

Fa la la, la la la, la la la. Troll the an - cient

yule - tide car - ol, Fa la la la la, la la la la.

See the blazing Yule before us,
  Fa la la la la, la la la la.
Strike the harp and join the chorus,
  Fa la la la la, la la la la.
Follow me in merry measure,
  Fa la la, la la la, la la la.
While I tell of yuletide treasure,
  Fa la la la la, la la la la.

Jingle Bells

J. P.

James Pierpont

Jin-gle bells! Jin-gle bells! Jin-gle all the way!

Oh, what fun it is to ride in a one-horse o-pen sleigh!

Jin-gle bells! Jin-gle bells! Jin-gle all the way!

Oh, what fun it is to ride in a one-horse o-pen sleigh!

Here Comes Santa Claus

Autry/Haldeman

*Gene Autry/
Oakley Haldeman*

Here Comes San-ta Claus, here comes San-ta Claus

Right down San-ta Claus Lane. Vix-en and Blit-zen and

all his rein - deer Are   pull -ing on   the   rein.

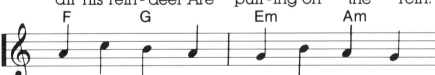

Bells are ring - ing,   chil - dren   sing - ing;

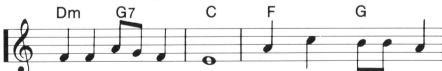

All is mer-ry and bright. Hang your stock-ings and

say your prayers 'Cause San-ta Claus comes to-night.

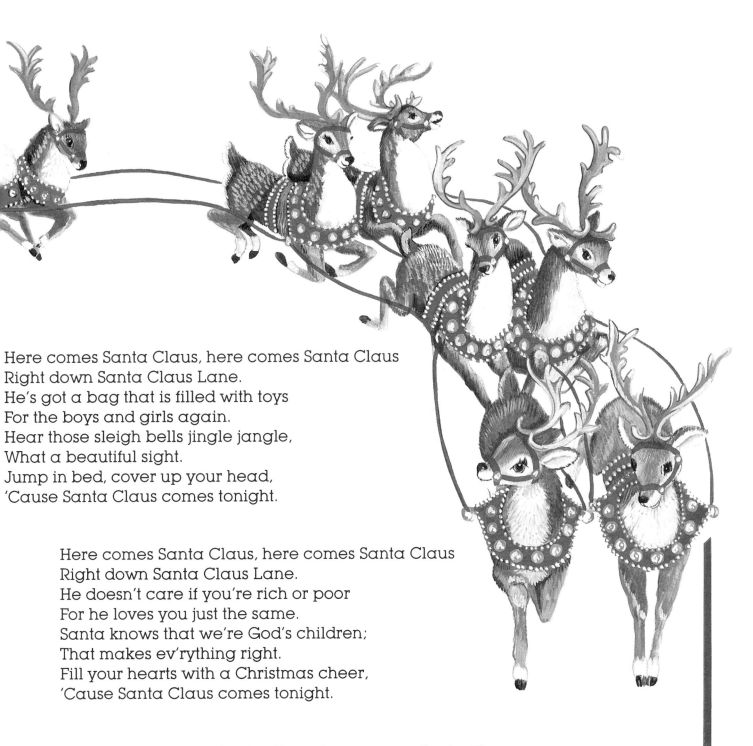

Here comes Santa Claus, here comes Santa Claus
Right down Santa Claus Lane.
He's got a bag that is filled with toys
For the boys and girls again.
Hear those sleigh bells jingle jangle,
What a beautiful sight.
Jump in bed, cover up your head,
'Cause Santa Claus comes tonight.

Here comes Santa Claus, here comes Santa Claus
Right down Santa Claus Lane.
He doesn't care if you're rich or poor
For he loves you just the same.
Santa knows that we're God's children;
That makes ev'rything right.
Fill your hearts with a Christmas cheer,
'Cause Santa Claus comes tonight.

Here comes Santa Claus, here comes Santa Claus
Right down Santa Claus Lane.
He'll come around when the chimes ring out;
Then it's Christmas morn again.
Peace on earth will come to all
If we just follow the light.
Let's give thanks to the Lord above,
'Cause Santa Claus comes tonight.

Up on the Housetop

Traditional

Up on the house-top rein-deer pause, Out jumps dear old

San - ta Claus; Down through the chim-ney with lots of toys,

All for the lit - tle ones' Christ - mas joys. Ho! Ho! Ho! Who would - n't go?

Ho! Ho! Ho! Who would - n't go? Up on the house-top,

click, click, click, Down through the chim-ney with good Saint Nick.

First comes the stocking of little Nell;
Oh, dear Santa, fill it well.
Give her a dolly that laughs and cries,
One that can open and shut its eyes.
Ho! Ho! Ho! Who wouldn't go?
Ho! Ho! Ho! Who wouldn't go?
Up on the housetop, click, click, click,
Down through the chimney
   with good Saint Nick.

Look at the stocking of little Will;
Oh, just see what a glorious fill!
Here is a hammer and lots of tacks,
Whistle and ball and a whip that cracks.
Ho! Ho! Ho! Who wouldn't go?
Ho! Ho! Ho! Who wouldn't go?
Up on the housetop, click, click, click,
Down through the chimney
   with good Saint Nick.

We Wish You a Merry Christmas

English

Oh, bring us a figgy pudding,
Oh, bring us a figgy pudding,
Oh, bring us a figgy pudding,
And bring it right here.

We all like our figgy pudding,
We all like our figgy pudding,
We all like our figgy pudding,
With all its good cheer.

We wish you a Merry Christmas,
We wish you a Merry Christmas,
We wish you a Merry Christmas,
And a Happy New Year.

Joy to the World

Isaac Watts
1719

Lowell Mason
1839

Joy to the world, the Lord is come; Let earth re-

ceive her King.   Let ev - 'ry   heart   pre-

pare Him room,   And   heav'n and na - ture

sing, And   heav'n and na - ture   sing, And

heav'n and   heav'n and na - ture   sing.

Joy to the world, the Saviour reigns;
Let men their songs employ;
While fields and floods, rocks, hills, and plains,
Repeat the sounding joy,
Repeat the sounding joy,
Repeat, repeat the sounding joy.

He rules the world with truth and grace,
And makes the nations prove
The glories of His righteousness,
And wonders of His love,
And wonders of His love,
And wonders, and wonders of His love.

Away in a Manger

German

A-way in a man-ger, no crib for a bed, The

lit-tle Lord Je-sus laid down His sweet head. The

stars in the sky, looked down where He lay, The

lit - tle Lord Je-sus a - sleep in the hay.

The cattle are lowing,
The poor Baby wakes,
But little Lord Jesus,
No crying He makes;
I love Thee, Lord Jesus,
Look down from the sky,
And stay by my cradle
Till morning is nigh.

Good King Wenceslas

John Mason Neale

Piae Cantiones
1582

Good King Wen-ces - las looked out on the feast of

Steph - en, When the snow lay round a - bout,

deep and crisp and e - ven. Bright-ly shone the

moon that night, though the frost was cru - el,

When a poor man came in sight,

gath - 'ring win - ter fu - el.

"Bring me flesh and bring me wine,
Bring me pine logs hither.
Thou and I will see him dine,
When we bear him thither."
Page and monarch forth they went,
Forth they went together,
Through the rude wind's wild lament
And the bitter weather.

In his master's steps he trod,
Where the snow lay dinted.
Heat was in the very sod
Which the Saint had printed.
Therefore, Christian men, be sure,
Wealth or rank possessing;
Ye who now will bless the poor
Shall yourselves find blessing.

Come All Ye Faithful

Frederick Oakeley

John Reading

O come, all ye faith-ful, joy-ful and tri - um-phant, O

come ye, O come ye to Beth - le - hem.

Come and be - hold Him, born the King of An - gels, O

come, let us a - dore Him, O come, let us a - dore Him, O

come, let us a - dore Him, Christ the Lord.

Sing choirs of angels, sing in exultation,
Sing all ye citizens of heav'n above.
Glory to God in the highest, glory!
O come, let us adore Him,
O come, let us adore Him,
O come, let us adore Him, Christ the Lord.

We Three Kings of Orient Are

J. H. H.

John H. Hopkins
1857

We three kings of Or-i-ent are, bear-ing

gifts we traverse a-far Field and foun-tain,

moor and moun-tain, fol-low-ing yon-der star.

O - star of won-der, star of might, star with

roy-al beau-ty bright, West-ward lead-ing

still pro-ceed-ing, guide us to the per-fect Light.

Born a Babe on Bethlehem's plain,
gold we bring to crown Him again;
King forever, ceasing never,
over us all to reign.
Oh, star of wonder, star of might,
star with royal beauty bright,
Westward leading, still proceeding,
guide us to the perfect Light.

Silent Night

Silent night, holy night,
Shepherds quake at the sight.
Glories stream from heaven afar,
Heavn'ly hosts sing, "Alleluia!"
Christ, the Saviour, is born.
Christ, the Saviour, is born.

Silent night, holy night,
Son of God, love's pure light,
Radiant beams from Thy holy face,
With the dawn of redeeming grace,
Jesus, Lord at Thy birth,
Jesus, Lord at Thy birth.

Merry Christmas
to all, and to all
a good night!